Courageous Captain

Courageous Captain

A Jataka Tale

Illustrated by Rosalyn White

DHARMA PUBLISHING

Jataka Tales Series

Second edition 2009, revised and augmented with guidance
for parents and teachers

Printed on acid-free paper

Printed in the United States of America by Dharma Press
35788 Hauser Bridge Road, Cazadero, California 95421

9   8   7   6   5   4   3   2   1

Library of Congress Conrol Number: 2009936421
ISBN 978-0-89800-515-8

www.dharmapublishing.com

Dedicated to
All the World's Children

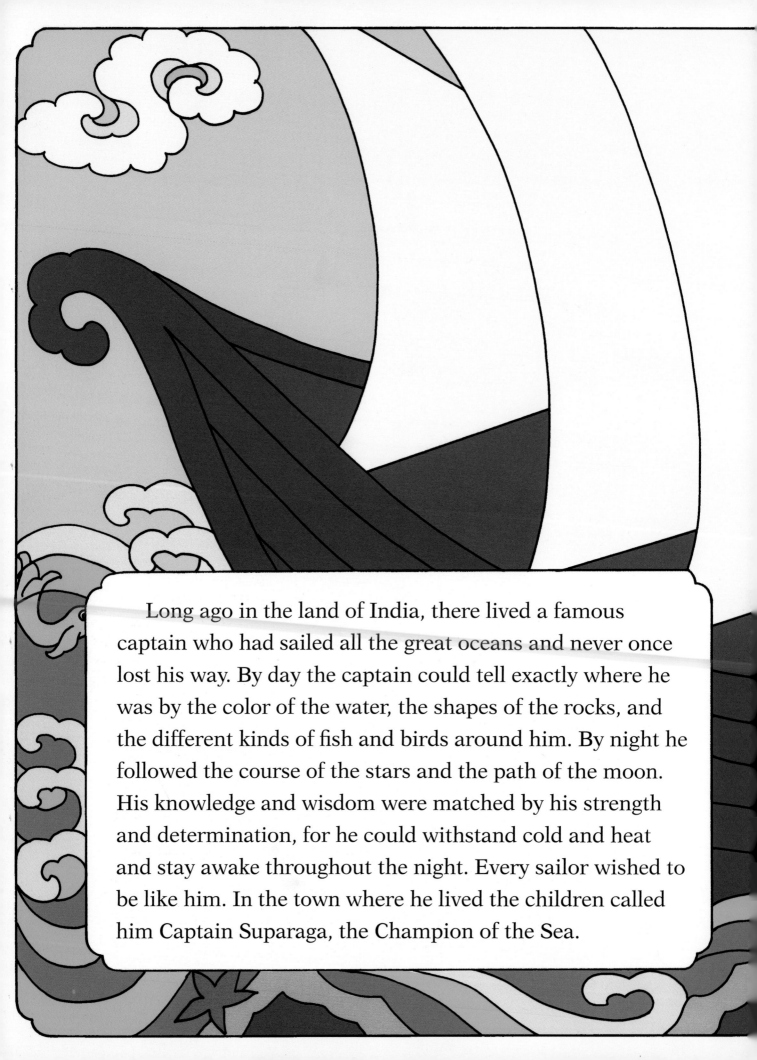

Long ago in the land of India, there lived a famous captain who had sailed all the great oceans and never once lost his way. By day the captain could tell exactly where he was by the color of the water, the shapes of the rocks, and the different kinds of fish and birds around him. By night he followed the course of the stars and the path of the moon. His knowledge and wisdom were matched by his strength and determination, for he could withstand cold and heat and stay awake throughout the night. Every sailor wished to be like him. In the town where he lived the children called him Captain Suparaga, the Champion of the Sea.

After many years at sea, Suparaga's eyes had grown weak and he could no longer pilot ships. But his reputation was legendary and one day two merchant sailors approached the old captain, asking him to join their crew.

"Please, great sir, accompany us on our first journey to the distant Land of Gold. Our sailors are keen but inexperienced, and they would feel safer with you on board. Your very presence will bring us good luck. We expect no work from you. Just join our ship!"

Out of compassion for the new crew, Captain Suparaga, though old and ailing, boarded the vessel and they set sail.

When the shore had long disappeared from view and
they had entered the open seas, the ship reached a stretch
of ocean called the Sea of Serpents where precious gems lay
hidden in the depths. The waves there shone with a brilliant
blue luster as if set aglow by the heat of the sun's beams.

Suddenly the wind was churning the water white,
whipping up a terrible storm. By sunset huge blue-black
clouds rolled across the sky like dragons, roaring thunder
and sending forth crackling flares of lightning. Rising and
falling on mountains of waves, the ship trembled and rocked
throughout the night. Still the crew was untroubled, feeling
certain that luck would be with them because the famous
captain was on board. On they dreamed of gold and jewels.

For days the wind and sea ran high and the ship was forced farther and farther into the open waters. Huge fish shaped like warrior demons in green armor were chasing after the ship. Now the sailors grew anxious, and panic began to take hold. Captain Suparaga spoke firmly, saying, "Storms and strange sights are natural on the great ocean. Remember that fear is not conquered by despair and low spirits, but by confidence and wisdom. Keep your focus and take control of the ship before it is blown further into uncharted waters."

But they did not turn the ship around, and before long they were surrounded by a silvery sea. The youngest sailor ran to seek the captain's advice. "You must be my eyes, boy, and describe exactly what you see. Then I can tell where the ship is heading," said the captain.

"The sea is bubbling with joy!" said the boy. "The surface is covered with fine foam and is shining like liquid moonbeams! This sea must be close to a land of miracles and riches!"

The captain replied, "This is the Milk Ocean. Tell your mates to take hold of the ship and turn it around right away."

But the crew watched the sparkling waters with fascination, their fears forgotten, and did not turn the ship around. Soon the youngest sailor hurried again to Captain Suparaga, describing the changing scenery: "The waves are a magnificent golden red, brilliant as liquid fire. Surely this must be an auspicious sign!"

The captain, however, knew exactly where the ship was headed. This ocean was close to the edge of the world and its red color reflected the great fires of the abyss. Knowing the crew would be terrified, he only said, "This is the Sea of Fire Garlands. Believe me; it would be wise to turn back immediately. Please attend to the ship and your tasks from now on!"

Some of the sailors finally heeded the captain's words, but their efforts were not enough. The ship was driven on by the winds and the water changed once again. "The sea is now glowing with the radiance of topaz. It looks friendly and calm," reported the youngest sailor dreamily.

"This is the Sea of Grass," warned Captain Suparaga. "Work harder! We must sail in the opposite direction." But no matter how they struggled, it was too late; they failed to gain control of the ship.

"The waters are colored deep green, like emeralds. This is the most wonderful sea of all!" exclaimed the youngest sailor. "But what is the soft roaring sound in the distance?"

Captain Suparaga sighed. "Alas, this is the Sea of Reeds just at the end of the world, before the waters fall crashing into a great abyss." He knew of only one way he might save the ship now, a way he did not call upon lightly. For the sake of the young crew, he stood upon the deck of the ship, threw his robe across his shoulder and spoke out loud to the sea and sky.

"Listen, spirits of the depths and spirits on high, and be my witness. In all my ninety years, I have lived with a pure heart. I cannot recall even one instance of having harmed any living being. May the power of this repeated kindness now be brought forth and turn this ship around."

Such was the power of the captain's life of pure action, so great the goodness of his heart, that at that moment he could take control of his fate and the destiny of others as well. Soon the sea calmed and the wind changed direction to blow the ship back the way it had come.

Seeing the ship's bow turn, the young crew rejoiced. They raised the sails and the ship glided over the water as gracefully as a swan. Now the captain spoke these mysterious words to the crew: "Each night cast your nets wide and load the ship with sand and rocks."

The sailors were puzzled but obeyed the captain. For five nights they filled their nets with rocks and sand. When the ship reached port, the crew offered thanks to the old captain, for although they had not reached the Land of Gold, they had returned with their lives.

When the young men unloaded the ship they found the hold filled with treasure – gold, silver and sapphires from the depths of the seas.

"Oh captain!" exclaimed the youngest sailor. "What fools we were to rely on good luck, instead of wise actions! If we had controlled the ship and ourselves instead of giving in to wild hopes and fears, we would never have been in such peril!"

Captain Suparaga understood this truth: practice kindness, wisdom and calm courage in all that you do and the power of good action will protect you.

The Jataka Tales nurture in readers young and old an appreciation for values shared by all the world's great traditions. Read aloud, performed and studied for centuries, they communicate universal values such as kindness, forgiveness, compassion, humility, courage, honesty and patience. You can bring these stories alive through the suggestions on these pages. Actively engaging with the stories creates a bridge to the children in your life and opens a dialogue about what brings joy, stability and caring.

Courageous Captain:
A Story About Finding True Treasure

Young men in search of treasure beg a famous captain who is retired and nearly blind to accompany them to a fabled land, hoping his presence will bring them good luck. But their adventures while crossing dangerous seas teach them that wisdom and good actions are more reliable than hopes and fascination.

Key Values

Respect for elders
Listening to experienced advice
Effective leadership
Reliability

Bringing the story to life

You might engage the children by saying, "In this story a ninety-year-old, highly skilled but nearly blind sea captain is asked on a voyage by sharp-sighted but young sailors who want to find treasure. What do you think might happen?" Then suggest, "let's read the story to find out."

- What did the sailors know about the captain?
- Why did the sailors want the captain to go with them?
- What kinds of seas and weather did they find when they sailed?
- Why was the ship in danger?
- How did the captain finally save the sailors?
- What did he say was the secret of his success?

Discussion topics may vary and questions can be modified depending on the child's age.

Teaching values through play

Follow up on the storytelling with creative activities that explore the characters and values and appeal to the five senses.

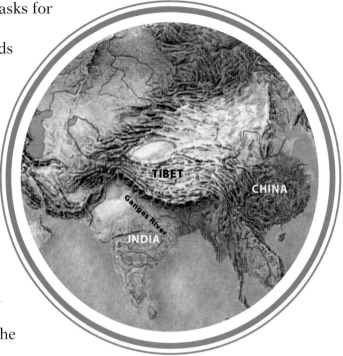

- Have children construct and decorate character masks for Captain Suparaga and several of the sailors.
- Have the children retell the story in their own words from the point of view of one of the young sailors. Then have them remember a time when they needed help learning something, like riding a bicycle or telling time. How do you think a captain knows direction at sea?
- Have them act out different parts of the story.
  1) Pick a section where the sailors don't follow the captain's experienced lead, and follow with a discussion.
  2) Let those playing sailors be the "eyes" of the captain, while one child can have his eyes covered. Pick a familiar place that does not contain hazards, and have the youngest sailor lead the captain. Have them carefully guide with directions such as "there is a bump here" or "feel the chair in front of you."
- Have the children close their eyes, and place three or four rocks on the table: fool's gold, a geode that hasn't been opened yet, and perhaps another rock containing a valuable mineral. When the children open their eyes, ask them which they like best. And then, which has the most value?

Active reading

- Before children can read, they enjoy storytelling and love growing familiar with the characters and drawings. You can just show them the pictures and tell the story in your own words with characteristic voices for each character.
- By reading the book to children two or three times and helping them recognize words, you help them build vocabulary.
- Carry a book whenever you leave the house in case there is some extra time for reading.
- Display the key values on the refrigerator or a bulletin board – at child's eye level – and refer to them in your daily interactions.
- Integrate the wisdom of this story during challenging times of chaos and confusion (perhaps even during very bad weather). Ask: What would the captain do? Which of his strengths would he call upon? You and the children can recall together the captain's skills, which we learn about at the start of the story.
- Talk about the story with your child while engaged in daily activities like cooking or driving. When driving, ask children to point out landmarks. This tale can help them become good observers and heighten their ability to read signs.

We are grateful for the opportunity to offer these Jataka tales to you. May they inspire fresh insight into the dynamics of human relationships and may understanding grow with each reading.

These adaptations of Jataka Tales are for children aged three to eight

JATAKA TALES SERIES